A ROOM TO LIVE IN

TAMAR YOSELOFF was born in the U.S. in 1965. Her first collection, *Sweetheart* (Slow Dancer Press, 1998) was a Poetry Book Society Special Commendation and the winner of the Aldeburgh Festival Prize. She received a New Writers' Award from London Arts for her second collection, *Barnard's Star* (Enitharmon Press, 2004). In 2005 she was Writer in Residence at Magdalene College, Cambridge, as part of their Year in Literature Festival. She is a tutor for The Poetry School and the poetry editor for Art World Magazine. She divides her time between London and Suffolk, and is currently working on her first novel.

Tamar Yoseloff

A ROOM TO LIVE IN

A KETTLE'S YARD ANTHOLOGY
Edited by Tamar Yoseloff

SALT

CAMBRIDGE

PUBLISHED BY SALT PUBLISHING
PO Box 937, Great Wilbraham, Cambridge CB21 5JX United Kingdom

First published 2007

Printed and bound in the United Kingdom by Biddles Ltd, King's Lynn, Norfolk

Typeset in Swift 10 / 12

ISBN 978 1 84471 420 9 hardback

Salt Publishing Ltd gratefully acknowledges
the financial assistance of Arts Council England

1 3 5 7 9 8 6 4 2

' "A Room to Live in" is a subject which we all have to consider either for ourselves or by letting other people consider it for us, and for each one of us who think for ourselves the answer will be different. You will be ready to say that we all live in rooms—but is this true? Do we really live in them? For how many of us is our room the expression of ourselves, so that when we go into it it just receives our natures, giving us a sense of ease and freedom?'

from a BBC radio broadcast,
given by JIM EDE, 28th November 1931

Contents

Foreword

KETTLE'S YARD BEGAN its life when, in 1956, H.S. 'Jim' Ede came to Cambridge, looking for 'a great house' where he and his wife, Helen, could live and where he could introduce his ideas about living spaces, and the role that art could play in them, to successive generations of students.

Ede had set out wanting to become an artist, but at a young age had found himself effectively the first curator of modern art at the Tate Gallery. It was during those years in the 1920s and '30s that he formed the basis of the collection that was to become Kettle's Yard, largely through friendships with artists such as David Jones, Ben and Winifred Nicholson, and Christopher Wood, but also through the acquisition of the estate of Sophie Brzeska which made him the prime holder of the work of Henri Gaudier-Brzeska.

For twenty years he and Helen lived first in Morocco and then in France before returning to England to fulfil his 'quixotic scheme'. Cambridge could not provide the stately home he sought and instead he adopted a row of all-but derelict cottages nestling beneath St Peter's Church. In little time the cottages had been remodelled as a single house and Jim had begun to open his door to afternoon visitors.

The Edes lived here until 1973 before retiring to Edinburgh. In the meantime Kettle's Yard had become an institution of the University and Jim's ambitions for a great house, where music would also play a part, had been achieved with the addition of Sir Leslie Martin's extension. Since then, Kettle's Yard has continued to grow with an expanding exhibition gallery as an essential foil to the house and there are plans for an education wing to come.

But the house, itself, remains as Jim Ede's unique creation, continuing to enchant and inspire visitors, continuing to ask questions about where and how we live. Periodically we ask artists to bring new work into the house, to introduce new observations and pose new questions. Here we have an anthology of prose and poetry to do the same.

We are deeply grateful to all these writers who have responded with such generosity and creativity to our invitation, to Chris Hamilton-Emery at Salt for so readily agreeing to publish, and to Tamar Yoseloff who has literally given herself over the last months to compiling and editing this rich tribute to a much loved place.

MICHAEL HARRISON
DIRECTOR, KETTLE'S YARD

Introduction

THERE IS A house in Cambridge where you can tug the bell pull and pass through a thick wooden door. You are welcomed by a woman who is not the mistress of the house, but who is at home there. You wander through room after room of paintings and objects, but it is not a museum. You are allowed to sit in the chairs, to take the books from the shelves. There are windows which let in the light, but somehow block out what is beyond. There are no clocks—you may lose track of time.

And so it is for the new visitor to Kettle's Yard. I still recall my first experience, sometime in the early nineties. I had visited Cambridge before, always marvelling, in the usual fashion of the American tourist, at its architectural gems, its handsome authority. Several people had told me to go to Kettle's Yard, had told me about its eccentric layout, its seminal collection of European modernist art. I had an inkling that it would be my sort of place. And it was. And so unlike anywhere else in that city of austere, imposing structures. I remember standing for a long time in front of David Jones's *Quia per Incarnati*, buying a card of it to put on my wall. Over the years, I returned there whenever I had a reason to travel to Cambridge. The house was never the same, changing as it does in different conditions of light and weather, but the experience was always uplifting.

In 2005 when I arrived at Magdalene College as newly-appointed Writer-in-Residence (to take my place in one of those austere structures) I went straight to Kettle's Yard, as a way of getting my bearings. I was fortunate enough to have worked with the artist Linda Karshan, who had exhibited in the gallery a few years before, and who put me in touch with

Michael Harrison. Michael greeted me warmly and said I should feel free to use the house whenever I wanted. And so I did. I spent so much time there that I established favourite chairs: the white armchair in front of the window in the Dancer room; the pale red chair in the Bechstein room, with a view out the window of the church. I wrote many poems in the house that autumn; they seemed to pour out of me without effort. And now when I return to Kettle's Yard, it is as if I am meeting an old friend again, and we fall into conversation where we left off. Once you have felt at home there, you are at home for life.

There are many stories like mine, many relationships established over the years, between that strange, maze-like jumble of a house, with its rare and beautiful objects (some rare and beautiful, some just beautiful) and the people who love it. So many of those relationships were fostered by Jim Ede, the owner of that remarkable house. He opened his doors to students and artists; lent works to those he knew would love them as he did; and educated a generation on how to appreciate what is essential, what is beautiful, not just in art, but in the world around them.

There are still many people in Cambridge who knew Jim Ede and who have stories of his generosity and passion. We are privileged that so many of them have contributed to this anthology. John Mole kept in touch with him for many years after he left Cambridge, and when Jim heard that John was working on a dramatisation of *In Parenthesis* with his sixth-form students, he insisted on setting up a meeting with David Jones (by then in a residential home in Harrow). Andrea Porter just knocked on the door one day, a curious fourteen-year old, and Jim invited her in and gave her a tour. He loaned a Gaudier-Brzeska drawing to Ian Patterson, then an undergraduate, who lived with it in his room for a term, and although he wasn't sure if he liked it, he felt bereft when it was finally returned. And Michael Bywater's fortuitous meeting with Jim just months before he left Cambridge for Edinburgh, left him questioning his youthful prejudices and gave him his first real lesson in how to look at art. It is particularly significant to have first-hand tales of Jim from those who knew him, as Kettle's Yard is a monument to him as much as to the artists he supported.

So many contributors touch on similar experiences, and their pieces form a dialogue. Fiona Sampson begins with the light trembling in a bowl on the windowsill, and Sarah Skinner charts its progress as it illuminates each object in its journey through the house. A perfect sphere of a pebble is passed from Jeremy Hooker to Jacob Polley. Neil Wenborn imagines the mariner Wallis at sea, and Fred D'Aguiar fashions a boat of dreams. And as John Greening evokes glass and Richard Burns speaks of marble, Martha Kapos praises stone. Some contributors pay tribute to individual artists, whose vision was as essential as Ede's in creating the house, such as Barbara Hepworth (Tony Curtis), Christopher Wood (Tamar Yoseloff) and Henri Gaudier-Brzeska (John Kinsella); where others, such as Anne Berkeley and Clare Crossman celebrate Ede as collector, 'the man who kept the light'.

Jane Duran and Sharon Morris, not content to settle on one experience, take us on a sensory tour of surfaces and forms. Ali Smith and Alan Bennett approach the house as a right of passage, a place to return to in different phases of life, for an understanding of the self. Sue Hubbard and Elaine Feinstein find a shelter against the cold, a place to make a migration, a pilgrimage. Meredith Bowles, David Hare and Rod Mengham all write of a source of inspiration which can be extended into other practices, like architecture or theatre or poetry. A way of seeing, a way of life; as Ruth Padel imagines the journey of the White Buddha, Susan Watson discovers purity of form in a Lucie Rie bowl, and Robert Vas Dias finds solace from the 'gimcrack world'. Perhaps Lawrence Sail puts it best, when he refers to the 'gift of attention', the way that the house forces us into silence, contemplation, recognition. This is Ede's gift to us.

We hope that this anthology repays that gift and stands as a suitable tribute to the first fifty years of Kettle's Yard. Long may it continue to inspire and thrive.

TAMAR YOSELOFF
LONDON, NOVEMBER 2007

A ROOM TO LIVE IN

ANNE BERKELEY

Monday

Try ringing the bell when nobody's there.
It gongs deep. You can hear
the shape of two pianos, spiral stairs, the thumbed harp
of Gabo, wheelback chairs; each plate and glass,
each stretched canvas reverberates
as your hand on the rope
hauls the house out of its dream
where a man gets up from his desk in welcome.

But the door stays black, shut, everything in place:
the bowls and charger on the mantel,
the bundled twigs in the grate, the patterned light
that fills the space he's risen out of.
You have interrupted him now:
he can never return to his bureau
writing cheques with a fountain pen to bring
the wind-stiff sailing ships leaning in to port.

FIONA SAMPSON

The Fire Glaze
Kettle's Yard, Cambridge

Begin with this thought
trembling
            on the brink of form,
the way light trembles
in a bowl on a window sill:

striking the glaze over and over
as if something might catch—
as if clay could break into flame—

As if a new world fires up
in each blink of your eye—
now it flickers to the blue bowl,
now snags on bright
jugsful of forsythia
                  or skids away
down the polished table—

Always at the back of your mind
the memory of faith;
that beautiful arrangement
in the bend of a lily
against dark oak.

~

Work is prayer,
and the woman cleaning these rooms
opens bright panes in waxed floorboards,
or between whitewashed rafters.

Her back records the tilt
of each oak plank and shelf.
She loves the shiny curve of one particular vase—
her wrist knows the distance from bowl
to maquette
              to the three egg-shaped stones
she puts straight
each Wednesday, at around eleven:

setting their symmetry to run again
until it runs down,
dusty and knocked.

ALAN BENNETT

from Untold Stories

from DIARIES: 2003

4 NOVEMBER. PASSING through Cambridge, we pay a ritual visit to Kettle's Yard. It's a house that never fails to delight and though there are features I don't like, it's a place I could happily live in. The attendants are mostly elderly and many of them seem to have known Jim Ede, whose house it was and who gave it and its art collection to the University in the 1970s.

One particularly sparky old lady recommends a video display running in the big room downstairs. At first it simply seems to be a slightly blurred record of a domestic interior: a kitchen, a sitting room with on the floor some toys including a couple of model planes. Suddenly one of these planes takes off, then another lands and soon the kitchen and dining room have turned into a busy international airport, planes crossing the room, landing on tables, taking off from work surfaces and all in total silence. They negotiate the narrow chasm of a slightly open door, deftly avoid a light fitting or a bowl of fruit and it's so absurd and silly I find myself grinning like a child. The artist, whose name I forget to write down, is Japanese and it's the last thing I'd ever have chosen to watch or expected to find in the austere surroundings of a house like this, but it's a delight.

AFTER I TOOK my degree I stayed on at Oxford to do research in medieval history, and also taught a little. I now had rooms in Merton Street, the back looking over to the Botanic Gardens. Some of my pupils were already collectors and possessed of a good deal more expertise than I ever had. David Bindman, later Professor of Art History at University College, London, was a pupil and would show me old master drawings he had picked up for a song, and another pupil, Bevis Hillier, later the biographer of John Betjeman and writer on the arts generally, would fetch along ceramics; I knew little of either and could neither confirm nor deny the confident attributions both boys put forward. But they taught me a more useful lesson than I ever taught them, namely that my own taste was for surfaces.

I was no collector. I cared more for the look of an object than for what it was. My aim was to make a room look interesting or cosy. I didn't see paintings as art objects so much as objects in a setting, and had the unashamedly English notion of pictures as furniture. I preferred them above tables, behind flowers, say, dimly lit by lamps or even half hidden by books. I would never want a room in which a painting was spotlit; it smacks too much of a museum, or a certain sort of gallery.

It is for these reasons that almost my favourite museum is the Fitzwilliam at Cambridge. It has too much on the walls and there is furniture besides, but it adds up to just the kind of inspired clutter that has always appealed to me. When I was stationed in Cambridge in the fifties I used to go there on Saturday afternoons out of term when the museum (and the town) was virtually empty.

The first room I would head for was on the right at the head of the stairs. There were some grand pictures but they were mostly English paintings then—a portrait of Hardy by Augustus John, some Constable sketches and Camden Town paintings and, presiding over them all, another Augustus John, a portrait of Sir William Nicholson. He's in a long thin black overcoat, hand outstretched resting on his stick, urbane, disdainful and looking not unlike the actor in the films of the time who played Professor Moriarty to Basil Rathbone's Sherlock Holmes. I didn't even know then that William Nicholson was himself a painter; what it was I admired was his detachment and his urbanity to the extent that the first chance I got I bought a thin secondhand black overcoat which made me look as spidery as he did.

If I like the Fitzwilliam for its clutter, I also like another Cambridge museum for its lack of it, though Kettle's Yard is not a museum at all but the home of Jim Ede, who gave it to the university in 1966. It caters to all my notions of art and interior decoration; the paintings (Ben Nicholson, Christopher Wood, Alfred Wallis), while individually delightful, are integral to the overall decorative scheme, even starting at the skirting board; nowhere else have I seen pictures hung so close to the ground. Jim Ede, too, thought that paintings were not always best seen undeflected: 'I remember how in Arezzo,' he writes, 'I went to see the Piero della Francescas, and saw nothing but an old faded curtain by an open window making shadows across the pictures.'

And so it is at Kettle's Yard, the paintings part of an assemblage and subject to the changing light. There's a mixture of old and modern furniture and though I don't always like the stones and objets trouvés on top of tables and chests (the decorative charms of pebbles and driftwood for me strictly limited) and though I would never paint a room white . . . here the whole house glows.

I would be happy to live in Kettle's Yard, feeling that if I did my life would be better, or at least different. It passes one of the tests of a congenial interior, that you feel you would like the food that is cooked there. At Kettle's Yard you can practically smell it.

JANE DURAN

Objects in Kettle's Yard

'We all want space—we are spatial beings . . .'
—JIM EDE

See where I go with this one.
There are so many spaces
to choose from: polished wood

as if the wind had made it,
were making it what it is;
alabaster birds, stones, a dancer

like a day given up for me.
Almost I went there:
all the way across a mountain plain

where the spaces restore and even out,
yet continuously entangle me;
so a glimpse of simplicity and order

in this quiet house must be a yearning
for something even more open—
a sheen from the wild, and to know

what I am reaching forward a little into:
a word, say, or a conversation that passes
untroubled right across a valley

as if it were happening in the next room
and the door wide open, a few visitors
caught together in the sunlight—

so much of it here, and restraint.
Wanting to see, to see, to see in time,
but never to lose that human warmth.

RICHARD BURNS

from 'Manual'

Notice the statue's hands how caringly
he tucked and folded chisel into marble
to free those moulded fingers from the stone
that would have locked them still and undiscovered
in solid dark like prehistoric bones

had not his own hands risen and in patience
spoken to stone by touch and by their probing
subtle persuasion coaxed those perfect fingers
out of their sheaths and for surrounding rock
substituted charged air and vision and history

The Geode

Listen well to the stone:
it releases its bang in the dust
like a statement of fact.

But let's make this
blunt stone into a brain.
Let's make its small

geography light up
like Vienna at twilight
in an ambience of meadows and emerald air.

Let's make it into a yellow
honeycomb of streetlit squares
celled in quiet.

The eye is speechless
as it moves among the resplendent
many-sided gabled houses

and crystal-pointed chimneys
pushed up one by one
like pencils

where even a geologist
meditating
over a packet of cigarettes

would be lost
in the cobbled back streets
of the intelligence.

JOHN GREENING

Glass

to take our transparency
and draw it out

of the bolt that welded
the desert sand

into a vessel for flowers
or for the lips

or with a breath into
blue hollow-ware

or in a square
reflect on the passing

hub running its lodes
out of silica fen

JOHN MOLE

Aquamarine

How blue glass catches light
to bottle it, then spills
in a drizzle of Chinese whispers
and the secret's out. You can hear
so many voices but the one you listen for
is lost among them. It contains
its own reflection as a man
might hold a snowing globe
and make a wish for us all
or wonder at the image of an echo
bounced back innocently
from his childhood, mirrored
by ethereal waves, familiar
yet distant as the moon.

Ian Patterson

Kettle's Yard

WHEN I WAS seventeen I spent the summer after I left
school, before I went up to Cambridge, in Italy. During those
three months in Florence I was to learn the language, get to
know the country, and attend a series of courses on Renaissance art and culture at the British Institute. This would help
me become a cultured individual, someone who knew about
art and civilisation. Someone who'd read Jacob Burckhardt
and could talk convincingly about Michelangelo or Masaccio.
It was my first real encounter with cultural history, and it
was quite an intensive one. I knew nothing about the painting and sculpture of the Renaissance before I went, and had
certainly never spent so much time looking at paintings,
frescoes, churches, museums, palaces and statues. Nor had I
ever drunk so much wine. The whole thing was a sort of intellectual finishing school for middle class students, and
decidedly Forsterian in its outlook. I lapped it all up with
determined enthusiasm, and came home feeling appropri-
ately superior. I'd started painting, too, views of Florence
and the surrounding countryside mostly, and thought I
might become a painter as well as a poet. Then, when I came
back to England, I discovered a series of talks on the Third
Programme by Isaiah Berlin, about German Romanticism,
which intensified my interest in cultural movements and the
roles art and poetry played in them.

I went up to Cambridge that October, two months after
my return, my mind full of systems, patterns, and inter-
connections. I was making a large-scale map of European

15

intellectual history from the medieval period to the present. Literary history (via Legouis and Cazamian's history of English Literature), art history, and the history of ideas were the framework into which I set about trying to fit the meaning and purpose of art. So when I first visited Kettle's Yard, in late 1966 or early 1967, it was a curiosity from another world entirely. No large vistas, no long perspectives, no story of cultural development. Quite the reverse. It was poky and quaint and unnervingly different from the story I'd been piecing together. It was quietly welcoming, of course, and there was a Kindly Old Gentleman to show one around or answer questions if need be. But I found that rather unsettling. For a start, it meant the questions had to be individual, had to arise from the experience of seeing things without an intellectual context. I wasn't used to that, and wasn't at all sure that my untutored reactions wouldn't be dismissed or ridiculed. So I said very little, and hoped not to be asked anything. I'd never encountered Art in domestic surroundings, unless you counted renaissance palaces. And Kettle's Yard didn't seem to be about the same sort of patronage as that. The rather ramshackle accumulation, as I saw it, seemed more to do with peaceful coexistence than hierarchical power. It was also a great deal more inviting than anything I'd seen in Italy. You could sit in quite comfortable chairs. You could read, or just gaze. Nobody moved you on. And actually it made you think. Not many people went there, either, so it was more like a private space than a gallery.

I can't recall what I made of the paintings at first. Did I like Alfred Wallis? Probably not. Or Ben Nicholson? Or Barbara Hepworth? I imagine I just didn't know what to do with them. For all its virtues, my education had not provided me with the confidence to know what I thought. In fact, it had overlaid my initial responses with worries and expectations and uncertainties which pretty much stopped me seeing what was in front of my eyes. I was quite at home in the grand narratives of intellectual and cultural history, happy to generalise about Humanism or Romanticism, or to talk glibly about individual poems, but I didn't really know what I was seeing when I looked at a modern painting. So reading or gazing or sitting in Kettle's Yard was more a matter of absorption than of attention. But out of it some kinds of attention did develop.

Looking back, it's easier to see what was going on. It's also easier to fit it into a larger cultural perspective. At the time I was rather puzzled for a while. I didn't go back to Kettle's Yard immediately, but did revisit it quite often during my first two years as an undergraduate. No epiphanies occurred, but I developed certain fondnesses. The light on arrangements of stones, for example, blue-ish in early summer and yellow in autumn made me look at things more attentively. And I got interested in David Jones, whose *In Parenthesis* I'd been reading. I borrowed a Gaudier-Brzeska drawing for a term, which I didn't particularly like at the time but which left me oddly bereft when I had to return it. I found myself trying to arrange my rooms in a slightly Kettle's Yard-like way, with flowers and found objects. How far this was a direct response to it and how far it was mediated through Habitat and contemporary design, I don't know. The late sixties saw the beginning of a movement of convergence between Jim Ede's taste and popular design which has continued until now the two are (superficially) almost the same, linked in that horrible term 'lifestyle'. But then it was, or I thought it was, new and strangely attractive; pictures, glass, china, stone, and wood showed their nature in a way I hadn't previously been aware of. Phrases like 'function and form' started to make more sense to me. I began to notice light, and colour. Even without the paintings, Kettle's Yard contained the sort of magic that belonged to houses I'd once read about in children's books. There was something about it that was the opposite of uncanny. Not—not ever—homely, but liable to make you forget about time while you were there.

Then in my third year I took against it. I didn't want to forget time, I wanted to feel the pressure of time, the nature of injustice, the clash of classes and the immorality of privilege. The house suddenly looked smug and aloof, its concerns small and inadequate to the world I was becoming aware of. I stopped going. I wanted to find art in the streets and in more declamatory forms of action. I think what I really disliked about the house was its testimony to a settled life and to a certain set of civilised values. A kind of closedness. It didn't seem equal to combatting the American war in Vietnam, it seemed too *private*. Not equal either to the more jagged or unbuttoned forms of music and poetry that were around at the end of the sixties. Yet it must have been something of a symbolic rejection, a parricide of some kind, because my enthusiasms and attitudes were full of inconsistencies. At the same time as I was rejecting the meditative quietness of Kettle's Yard, I took up buddhism for a few months (its new popularity another by-product of the Vietnam war) as well as marxism (which lasted longer). A passion for Elizabethan poetry and music coexisted with a variety of forms of mildly dissident behaviour (not going to any supervisions was one, going barefoot was another), as well as with editing a poetry magazine the name of which was taken from (and chosen by) the *I Ching*. So in turning against Kettle's Yard I may have been making it a scapegoat for complications in my own life. But whatever the rationale, it was several years before I went back.

By the time I went back again, things had changed. The gallery had been added, and changes made to the house. I had changed, too. I'd learned a lot of stuff in the intervening period. I knew a great deal more about modernism and abstraction and painting, and about the artists themselves and about the historical period their work came out of. The various aspects of the collection fitted together intellectually in a way that I couldn't have imagined in the 1960s. At the same time, in some not completely tangible way the house had changed from a live collection to a memorial, a museum. By virtue of expansion and contraction on both our parts, it had become manageable. It had also become part of my own past, partly absorbed, partly not. Now, after almost thirty more years, it's hard to resist the rosy glow of a largely invented nostalgia.

The thing is, it took some years for the point of Kettle's Yard to sink in properly. I may have been inhabited by more contradictions than most undergraduates were in the late sixties, but not I think hugely so. I was certainly torn between possible selves, or at least activities, a lot of the time, but that's part of growing up. One of the first things I'd abandoned when I got to Cambridge was the idea that I might be a painter—by the time of my first visit to Kettle's Yard I was already clear about that. Then I stopped acting. I changed the kind of clothes I wore, and the people I hung out with. I never lost my interest in grand intellectual systems, cultural history, patterns of influence and all that sort of thing, but my encounters with Kettle's Yard eventually shifted the focus of that interest on to the materials themselves and their forms. I continued to read Ruskin and Pater as well as Herbert Marcuse and Guy Debord, and continued to puzzle over the relation of art to things and to history and politics, and to worry about what poetry was really for. But always now with a closer reference to the process of production itself. I began to think about these things in terms of ideas that had got into my mind in Kettle's Yard, ideas about matter, materials, permanence and ephemerality, and how looking relates to seeing. In fact that was when I started to get some distant sense of the extraordinary complexity of the whole simple business of casting light on things.

NEIL WENBORN

In Memory of Alfred Wallis

what i do mosley is what
use To Bee out of my own
memery what we may never
see again as Thing are altered
all To gether Ther is nothin
what Ever do not look like
what it was sence i can Rember

— ALFRED WALLIS: letter to Jim Ede, 6 April 1935

He still works it, the sea. Whatever
    comes to hand—offcuts of signage,
boxes the grocer saves, a calendar—
    brings it with all its cargo

thronging his parlour. Scrap
    and salvage shape his recollection.
Rag and bone man, mariner,
    widower now, he paints for company.

~

Real paint too: yacht paint. *Not like
    them London ones.* Loam browns and kelps,
hummock and rockweed green;
    gull grey, pebble grey, the scumbled white

of wavecrests, the gunmetal
      inshore, bible black—
it all comes back, a Cornwall out of memory.
      what i do mosley is what use to Bee

      ∼

Porthmeor. Porthminster. He cleaves to the known,
      his register—Hayle Bay, Godrevy,
Smeaton's Pier, Saltash, Hamoaze—
      a listing towards

the lost. It comes up
      vivid as a child's dunked stone
or his first voyage—Devonport, Labrador—
      his every which way faring.

      ∼

The irretrievable
      liberates all perspectives. Absence
draws him like the Godrevy light
      casting its net of colours

seaward, landward,
      seaward again. His mind
reels like a compass, homing.
      What you see now you see all points at once.

      ∼

Dead reckoning
    charts his St Ives, its set and drift.
At Back Road West there are ships in motion
    on every surface—ships and houses

unanchored as ships. Even the lighthouse
    trails its wake of rocks like a seabird
cornering as it lands,
    skidding to plane a chute of white water.

    ~

He trims more card. Under his brush
    the Cornish firelight dips and yaws.
Seventy years out, in the deep grounds
    the waves are thundering, a cabin boy

steadies his eye on the horizon.
    Berthed in the past, even so long
ashore dry land upends
    his bearings, the here and now still pitches under him.

Note: In navigation, *dead reckoning* is a method of determining one's present position based on a known past position when direct observations are
impossible.

CLARE CROSSMAN

Fiddle-fish and Wave at Kettle's Yard

They came to him the man who kept the light,
the tesserae of coasts, the shells and rocks,
the smoothed wood and the stones.
They brought letters printed on cloth,
boats from a children's storybook,
the stern lines of winter trees, the holiness of flowers.
It was easy. There was no contradiction between
the waves arc, the fall of clay, marble on a rope
moving like the liquid silver scales of a fish,
everything had a rhythm and a flight.

He collected sculpture, paintings to settle
on the plain surfaces of his house,
amongst the smell of cooking, the turn of pages,
slate and the creaking of stairs.
Underneath the surface: a basic shape of bone,
outlines of legs and face, arms to reach, cradle or kill,
celebrate and dance, hold up the air.
As well to be émigré, in a pair of worn out shoes.

He knew those artists from his journeys,
on trains and planes, amongst all shades of colour,
east and west. Reaching to touch those things,
which make us human: a naked eye the edge of the world,
believing in the power of dreams.
What better than to open windows, treasure glass,
leave us with a question about stars?
Every day they echo, what he left with cornflowers:

an image of their fragile blue and the sun's blazing.
The essence of what we half already know:
these surfaces of oil, copper scraped to make
the outlines of a cat, the glint of horses' heads,
details of wings. Everything sacred to the ground,
and God with many names.

Fred D'Aguiar

Dreamboat

A ship sailed
through my body:
my ribs for rigging,
my lungs for sails,
my backbone
for a main mast.
All my cargo
were children
of the middle
passage, bound
for slavery, or an
unceremonious
burial at sea—
all this in my one
landlocked body.

I tried to steer
the ship back
to the slave coast
by sheer will,
my skull for a bridge,
my hands lashed
to the wheel,
my eyes a crow's nest
searching for Africa's
ziggurat coast.

My legs kicked,
my arms pulled,
my lungs filled.
I was food for fish.
I sank in clouded deep.
The ship sailed on.

The Artist
(i.m. Christopher Wood)

Over rooftops, drunken
chimneys   (a bird's-eye view

of lovers throwing punches,
whores in red chemises)

you are waiting   for the sky
to find its pure cerulean.

Your brush is raised,
                    your eye
fixed on a view beyond the frame,
your pipe (which *is* a pipe)
unlit
        until the picture's finished.

Across town
Picasso takes Marie-Thérèse
to pieces,
        Cocteau drowns
in absinthe. *Vert.*

Verité.

You can no longer see yourself.
You must be sick
        like the men
who lie with *les petites Chinoises*
in dragon gowns
                billowing
the smoke of a thousand dreams.

The brave land that you knew
    (the sailboats and cliffs)
gives way to this *ville désolée*.

Somewhere in the distance
    a train
steams full ahead (an angry bull,
a woman screaming).
        You will meet it
straight on.

Kettle's Yard

They say that the representation of the human form is the wellspring of Western art. I have to believe what They say because not only do I not know much about art, I don't even, to be honest, know what I like. But it makes sense. Those little men on cave walls, showing what they can do, or what they would like to do; the Renaissance grandees, demonstrating their status; heavy Victorian masters-of-colleges, weighed down by knowledge and *gravitas*; the faces of Roman emperors, stamped into coinage, transmitting, like some early television, the head of the *capo di tutti capi* into the furthest corners of the empire so that right up to the hinterlands of Ultima Thule, beyond the reach of geography or the rule of law, men at their daily business would look upon his image and know their place.

They also say that art, like all excess beyond the survival-ists' quadrivium—water, shelter, food and A Plan—is about sexual attraction; our art, like our intelligence, is a peacock's tail: *See my wonderful superfluity; now take off your clothes.* The limbless painters of Christmas cards may do it with their mouths, those without hands may do it with their feet, but, They say, in the end we all do it with that most wilful of organs, the ever-hopeful phallus. Maybe that's why through history, most art has been made by men. Or perhaps not. I don't know.

What I *do* know is that, in my case, sexual display and the human form were what drove me to art. A pretty poor sexual display, it's true, but the human form in question was as beguiling as they come, and I was a first-year undergraduate (Medical Sciences) who didn't really have a clue. I chose to manufacture a personality based on imitation and flat prejudice.

I have to say, I did pretty well. If I could recapture that first glorious flush of universal bigotry, I would be a happy man. It was *so* easy: all I had to do was take a quick look at something and instantly hate it: rock music, hippies, Gurdjeff, dramatic realism, Jane Austen, Methodism, lobster, cyclists, tweed, economics, politicians, Morris dancing, sportsmen, *everything*.

Including, of course, Kettle's Yard.

I don't recall how I came to hate Kettle's Yard. There was certainly nothing considered about my opinion. I simply *knew*, by some beastly osmosis, that it embodied Things I Hated. In retrospect, those Things probably included William Morris, vegetarianism, Folk Art, wattle, handlooms, hashish, batik, bards, plumbago, muesli, apple-bobbing, spiritualism and Virginia Woolf. 'Merrie England,' I thought to myself, 'Fruit juice. Aesthetes. Fabianism,' and, having thought so, relaxed into comfortably into hating Kettle's Yard.

And then came the human form. The wellspring of all art. Or, in my case, the wellspring of at least having a look at the stuff.

I had tried, in a desultory way, before, but the whole idea of a visual aesthetic escaped me. I couldn't draw; couldn't paint; couldn't, really, see any reason why anyone would want to do such things. Only in theory could I see why anyone would want to look at the result. In practice, painting and the plastic arts were closed to me and, given my virtuoso bigotry skills, I took the simple step of deciding that those who understood and valorized them were deluded.

The great galleries and museums made no inroads on my art-blindness. I was immune to the National, the Tate, the Wallace Collection, the Fitzwillian. They were *grandes horizontales*, aloof and, if beyond my cultural means, also beyond my cultural orbit. All I had to do was not go in.

But the human form—she was named after a flower— wanted to go in. She went in all the time. She had books of paintings and sculptures. She discoursed on Cubism and Fra' Angelico, on Duncan and Vanessa Bell and Paul Klee, and after a week or so I was on the point of hiding in the library and mugging up a hitherto-unrevealed passion for Watteau in order to advance my case. So when she suggested Kettle's Yard one afternoon ('It's wonderful! I go there all the time!') it was the work of a moment to turn my prejudices on a six-pence, cry 'Yes! I love it too! It's just that I've never actually *been* there!' and head off along Bridge Street.

I was alarmed when she rang the bell—I had hoped to sneak in, anonymously—and even more alarmed when we went in and there was Jim Ede.

The best-known photograph of Ede shows him rising from his writing-bureau, looking at the camera with the expression of a man about to come forward to greet a friend: eager to say hello, to show things, to talk. The photograph captures the man with forensic precision, but I found his appearance terribly alarming.

He wasn't supposed to be there.

Jim Ede was a name; a figure in a photograph; the *genius loci* of Kettle's Yard which was, in its turn, a three-dimensional archive to his memory. He had started Kettle's Yard. It had been his home. It was famous. He had given it to the University.

On all these counts, it was obvious: he had to be dead.

But there he was. Had I come a couple of months later, he and his wife would have moved to Edinburgh. But he was not in Edinburgh, and he was not dead.

I was about to lose face terribly, and I cast around me for something to say which would salvage the situation. He was chatting away to the flower-girl—unnervingly, we were the only people there—and the word 'Miró' emerged from the darkness. I had seen a Miró painting not long before—*The Concert on the Branch*—and been terribly pleased by it; this was painting I could vaguely understand. It was, to me, rather like music. I could feel its rhythms and tonalities; I might not be able to see it, but I could, in a way hear it.

'And what do you make of his work?' said Ede.

I was cornered, not least by the word 'his'. I had assumed that someone called Joan was a woman; I had pictured her as a frail, elderly but indomitable lady living in Barcelona with three cats, an aviary and a fondness for Cuban rum. His 'his' came as a shock, and I temporarily lost my grip on my pretensions.

'Gosh,' I said, 'I thought she was a woman, and I thought the picture was more like music but that might be because it said "concert" in its title and anyway I don't really know how to look at things but it made me smile in that sort of way where you're so glad that it's made you smile that you slightly want to cry. Sorry. I'm not very good at art.'

At which point I decided three things were going to happen:

(1) The flower-girl would walk away in contempt;

(2) Mr Ede would throw me out; and

(3) I would die of shame on the grass.

I was wrong on all three counts and enthralled and delighted by the responses of both the flower-girl and Jim Ede to what was perhaps my first honest and unpretentious utterance since puberty. It was many years before I could abandon my pretensions entirely, but I did take the first tiny step, under Jim Ede's . . . I was going to say 'tutelage' but it was more a pleasant chat between equals, one of whom was, however, far more equal than the other, towards learning how to look at art.

I still can't really do it, but at least I now know what I can't do. It will never be natural—I shall never be able to internalise my response to visual art—but I do know how to read it, even if it remains a conscious process. And that is probably thanks to Jim Ede. Had he sighed wearily or dismissed me as a fool, I should probably never have looked at a painting or a sculpture again, and my prejudices would have been confirmed. As it was, I slowly got the hang of looking, and, equally slowly, learned to distrust my own prejudices.

And, of course, discovered one of the greatest delights I know: the sheer joy of finding that I have been utterly mistaken about something. It has happened more times than I can count, since then, but every time I feel as if a door has opened. 'I was entirely wrong,' I say to myself; 'Good. Now we're getting somewhere'.

The experience didn't take, not immediately. The flower-girl decided she preferred a less ludicrous young man, and presently, after a set of abominable exam results, I gave up medicine, or, more accurately it gave me up.

I turned to the English tripos which offered me the chance to tart around being a thespian, musician and denizen of irrelevant sections of the University Library. This being the Seventies, and I being an irretrievably urban young man, my (partly bogus) fashionable preoccupations were those you would expect. I became—or posed as; it is hard to tell now—

a Maoist; I subscribed to *The Peking Review*, flirted with a gravelly, malodourous macrobiotic diet, adulated the 7:84 Theatre Company, read R.D. Laing and Elias Canetti, put several Cambridge organs at risk by playing Ligeti's hullucinatory, monstrous *Volumina*, owned a copy of *Taking Tiger Mountain by Strategy*, worshipped Artaud, Grotowski, Pierrot Lunaire and Hindemith, and became, overall, the sort of young man whom P.G. Wodehouse would have happily thrown to the Hosts of Midian.

But though, in life, we seldom find ourselves on the road to Damascus, and our epiphanies are subsumed into the carapace we grow to protect ourselves from the indignities of our ignorance, something had changed.

The encounter at Kettle's Yard had at least chiselled a chink in my shell; the scales did not fall from my eyes but one or two of them became perhaps a little less opaque; and I learned that being wrong, and saying so, was not a catastrophe. I went on being wrong (and went on being pretentious) but perhaps I knew, somewhere inside the shell, that that wasn't the end of the world either.

There can be few better or more important lessons. And I learned it from a man who had the most beguiling and crucial of the teacher's instincts: the capacity for delight coupled with the unstoppable desire to explain why he is delighted.

We live in the most obsessively-documented times in history. And yet all our digital photos, our online diaries, our FaceBook entries and Twitters and webcams and blogs fail entirely, most of the time, because they say nothing except 'I was here. I was here. And I was *here*.'

Jim Ede created a different archive in which he was the narrator but not the subject. The subjects of Ede's archives were—ostensibly, at least—Moore, Hepworth, the Nicholsons, Brancusi and the rest who inhabit what was once his home. But this archive, by a trick of reverse perspective, narrates Ede's life more eloquently than any biographer, any room full of papers, any hard disk with terabytes of digital images and video files. Kettle's Yard says, not 'I was here. I was here. I was *here*,' but 'Look at this! And this! And see this one? Well, it's . . .'

It is what you might call a meta-archive: a story about a man told through what he collected and loved. The story is embedded in the collection. Like all good stories, it goes on being told. And, like all good stories, it has a moral. The moral varies. I have said what it was for me. For you, it will be something else. But for all of us, Ede and Kettle's Yard re-state a precept to which it seems good, if hard, to aspire: *si monumentum requiris, circumspice.*

ROBERT VAS DIAS

After 'The Island (with constant chaos)'

'For Art & Science cannot exist but
in minutely organised particulars.'
—WILLIAM BLAKE

Flora in their motley pots array
    insouciant faces with sang-froid.

When she's not looking they creep
    closer and closer and sooner

rather than later completely
    infiltrate the remaining space

with their pinks and yellows and blues,
    intimidate her with showy beauty

their urge to deflower
    and propensity to fade into

decrepitude, enfold her
    memory mulching into entropy.

   ∾

My life she thinks is measured out
    in colourful pottery collected

in country village studio shops.
    'Dropping in' she's fired

by the hunt, asks to see the kiln,
    then retreats from that violent heat

spying the one-and-only
    on sagging shelves.

One has bred dozens, allotropic
    scenes, the torrid and the horrible,

painted glaze of moments
    savoured and as quickly lost.

    ~

How the bric-a-brac and
    décolletage clutter the concept.

Sometimes the sofa's the only place
    to think of sex and furniture

how randomised particulars press in
    and violate that private space.

She feels like hurling the crockery
    and pots across the room

but might hit the cat.
    Make straight a path

through the wilderness
    where one geegaw begets another.

Let me re-arrange the mugs and vases
    Spirit of the Dead Watching.

Come and get me, she whispers, before
    I perish of the gimcrack world.

Note: 'The Island (with constant chaos)' is the title of a painting by Stephen Chambers RA, who held a Fellowship at Kettle's Yard in 1998–9.

TONY CURTIS

Three Personages: Barbara Hepworth
at Kettle's Yard

Three figures stand together
in their long cloaks.
Three personages.

A representation or figure of a person.
Only three speaking personages
should appear at once upon the stage.

Two conspire
but the third leans back
as if in thought.

The road beneath their feet is wet
and reflects dangerously.
One step,

one step and it would be settled.
The space between their heads
will never be so close.

These clean and discrete,
crafted, standing stones are poised:
theirs is an arrangement. Stasis even.

Though the shining on which one
might slip
was never so treacherous as now:

The Three Wise Men
The Three Witches
Triplets.

ANDREA PORTER

Three Haiku for a Saint

seed becomes the tree
bowed to the insistent course
bent backed to heaven

a spark to the heart
the fierce act of creation
fired to glorify

fleshed by each dark step
the skin crazed as one branded
by nature to burn

Extension upper level, under the stairs. John Catto, found statue, a
burnt branch of a willow struck by lightning. Entitled 'Saint Edmund'
by Jim Ede.

RUTH PADEL

White Buddha at Kettle's Yard
For the poets, writers and composers of Rangoon and Mandalay

White Buddha, coarse-ground two hundred years ago
on Street of the Buddhas in Mandalay
where the Chinese have bought up everything
including the Swan Hotel, and no one born in town
can afford to live there. Where on Mandalay Hill
thirty years ago, you could see leopards. Now
you see sunset, jade dagger shadows in the dust
and young Mandalayans walking up over them
barefoot. Up through the pair of giant
lion-dragons, whisking marble pigtails

laughing snarling-gargoyle mouths
and guarding the gilded portal. Up past surveillance
cameras, all round, wherever-whoever-you-are.
Up, to escape the sweltering town
and talk, if they can, to tourists, exchange
precious stones of English and of French
for anything, anything from outside.
Up to the massy Buddha, pointing at
the Lion Palace in its moat of livid ripples
and albino tulle busby of heat mist.

Inside, as all citizens know, as blisters
and back aches show, are glass mosaic halls
of turquoise mirror, destroyed in World War II,
restored by their own forced labour.

43

No one enters now. Look, Gate of Ill Omen
where the old kings' condemned prisoners departed.
And Mandalay Correction Facility, soundproofed,
lit by rays of the red-set sun! Up to the one place
you can imagine feeling free, below a hedgehog
of old bone, the white pagoda prickling blue-fire sky,

to look far out to the crawling, hazy lavender silhouette
of dangerous Shan Hills, look down to the flat
silver tapeworm of the Irrawaddy—which, come
the monsoon, will cover emerald rice paddy in wet gleam
to the horizon. White Buddha, cut and sheened
on Street of the Buddhas in Mandalay,
where the regime felled all trees for surveillance
and now wants to grow them back. (You can go to jail
for cutting down a tree.) Where everyone smiles, everyone
is slender, men dandle babies, women walk safely alone.

Where ancient kings were burned in streets of their own
making, their ashes thrown in velvet reticules
into the Irrawaddy. Where no one has ever been free—
first there were those sex-crazed, gem-crazed kings,
then the British and Japanese, and now the junta.
White Buddha, roughed out on Street of the Buddhas
in Mandalay, where citizens have eight hours of electricity
in seventy two and memorize the rota in advance.
(Tourists never know, the air conditioning
in their hotels switches to generator, at once.)

Where 'The People's Desires' are written foot high
on walls, and stamped in every paper:
     Oppose those relying on external elements,

acting as stooges, holding negative views.
Oppose those trying to jeopardize
Stability of State, Progress of Nation.
Oppose foreign nations interfering
in internal affairs. Crush internal
and external destructive elements
as the Common Enemy.

Where writers have to pay to print this stuff
on the front page of their books. Where you see
living sparrows sold in shallow baskets,
delicate brown-mottle feathers brittle-broken,
fifty birds a go. You pay the old woman
to release them, gain merit in your next life,
a good deed fifty times over. They flutter off
but—starving, dehydrated—sink to earth
to be caught again. White Buddha, shaped
to your pedestal on Street of Buddhas

where fleets of new marble Buddhas, fifty metres high,
lie tipped on their back or side in salt-white chippings
round the corner from Lane of the Bamboo Fan-Makers,
Alley of the Makers of Hand-Beaten Gongs.
Where, in a hundred degrees of heat, we watched
the Goldbeaters of Mandalay, two shifts of eleven-
year-old boys pounding apricot sheets of gold
to gossamer goldleaf (thinner than ink
on a printed page) non-stop
like oars on a Hollywood slave ship.

And, in the inner room, little girls of eight
who should be learning the periodic table,

migrations of birds, distances between the stars,
packaged bright-crumbly goldleaf,
tiny fingers for tiny squares into ten-*kyat*
packets, sold to anyone who wants to gain merit
by layering gold on a Buddha. White Buddha, rubbed
down like a dream of salt on Mandalay's map
of limbo, where generals are photographed
opening pagodas too bright to look at

except far off or in the rain, their gold relayered
every year. Where a thousand *kyats* are a US dollar
and a prostitute working the boats up the Irrawaddy
can't face fifty *kyats* for a condom
but charges her clients fifteen. Where censorship
is an industry, its own large building says so,
and every word printed is vetted, 'Blossom falls
to the ground' is blacked out in magazines
because it might mean the student killed
in last week's demonstration. White Buddha, drilled

out of a block on the Street of Buddhas 1809
or thereabouts, under thrumming monsoon rain
before rubber flip flops were invented, among
elephants, palanquins, intrigue of royal wives,
delicate courtesans rotting in satin body bags
unseen behind the stupas of chalcedony,
quartz, opal, painted leogryphs and cobras.
White Buddha, prayed to in Mandalay
before the British came with axes for the teak forest,
cannon, a civil service, taxes, desperate women

and a military band playing 'Here I Pitch
My Lonely Caravan'. Before they deposed Thibaw,
King of Kings, and smashed the turquoise mirror.
Blood ran . . . White Buddha from Mandalay, now
angled on the top white shelf of a corner cupboard
by a vermilion-stoppered bottle flecked with gold.
White Buddha, one faint line of an embroidered strap
shallow-chiselled in your naked chest, scuffed
marble eyes, winged ear lobes reaching to your shoulders
leaving twinking holes, little epaulettes of light.

How those blue-gilded frills of fine bone china gleam
either side your hips, behind you, like cerulean
flounces on a mediaeval queen. Your left hand
calm on your lap with open palm,
right hand on your right thigh and hanging down,
middle finger touching earth for that moment when
you called the Earth to witness
you had reached the light
and Earth in a mighty roar agreed you had.
Buddha among the crockery, in a house

where stones, light, driftwood, even silence, sing
about holding on to what we are. Saying,
'I come from a place of wreck
you cannot possibly imagine.
A land where we always seem to lose
the long bronze battle for humanity. But something stays.
Listen to the breath of earth
rising to meet you at twilight. Don't be taken in
by surfaces. Be able to walk away from what you've made,
to give away what you love—

like this house, where every fold of cloth
upon a sofa casts a shadow smile
on parquet patterning; where light spreads
over woodgrain floor like pilgrims quilting goldleaf
on a Buddha. Choose stillness. Touch the earth.
Stay centred. Life is loss
but hey—not only loss. Walk away
from what has hurt. Don't let it stick
in your ear or in your throat,
a barbed seed-whisker of barley. Let go your As If—

as if always reproaching world for some big thing
not given. Give up the bullet you carry round
with you: the shard in your heart,
the flake of skin pulled off. Don't let
What-Might-Have-Been,
the fantasy where you are moonwave
through and through, always beautiful
in an always generous sea, translucent
as a mother-of-pearl butter-knife—
don't let, I say, the alternative,

the you-and-I-at-the-edge-of-foam,
stand in the way of loving what you have
and what you are. Be home ground. Say,
I am. Say, I am me and I am now.
Enjoy what's here to hand,
this whirl-snake of sea-stones
picked from sand and graded into spiral.
Curling in or curling out? You choose.
Be the moment of your life. How you see
is how you live. Choose me.'

MEREDITH BOWLES

One Summer

I REMEMBER THE moment when I first made a painting that was about what I *felt* rather than what I *saw*. I was about 23 years old, and prior to this prided myself on my artistic competence and knowledge of Art. My watercolours were informed by my appreciation of Cotman, my illustrations drew inspiration from Dufy. When I went to galleries I tried to guess the artist without reading the labels. Mentally I was able to catalogue movements of art as I walked around.

The painting I made (it was not much good, by the way) had a repeated print of a bone that I had found, with the image floating over a background of rust colours and ochres. Suddenly I felt a flood of associations; the bone was picked up on a walk in the Wicklow mountains in Ireland, amongst the peat bogs. It connected me to all the mountains I had ever walked on, to the sheep in the Cumberland fells, to the russet colours of autumn ferns. The earth colours reminded me of archaeological excavations, and the ferns of pre-history, and to camping as a child. It contained for me both emotion and meaning, allowing me to place myself more fully in my present life, as well as seeing myself within geological time.

It was a revelation. I did loads of the prints and paintings, starting to see them as 'Celtic landscapes', and began to clarify what they could be about. Some of them I got to sell, and so began to see myself as a painter. The real value in the discovery, though, was to bring about a way of seeing things that related to *experience* rather than *knowledge*. I started going to art galleries able to carelessly dismiss paintings that didn't interest me, preferring to look at things that moved me. I gave up the habit of 'ticking off' paintings in my head, and grew more contented with my patchy knowledge. I realised that feeling bad about having a poor knowledge of Art was not half as much value as feeling good about discovering paintings that I liked.

~

As an undergraduate student (before the expedition into Art), I had attacked Architecture in the same way as I had approached Art. I was able to design well, with references to Movements in architecture that demonstrated my knowledge and passion for the subject. Like many student projects, mine too were brimming with ideas and full of idealism. Leaving college, my friends and I started a firm. We called it The Finsbury Plan, named after an ambitious urban plan for Finsbury in North London (a few of the blocks of flats and the health centre were realised, in 1938). We designed punk pads for city boys, baroque exhibitions at The Royal Academy, a swimming pool in Devon, with a gold mosaic motif as if the black rock had fissured and filled with water. Here we were, out there and doing it, doing it all.

Soon after this I applied to the Architectural Association to complete my studies. I was interviewed by the legendary head of school, Alvin Boyarsky. He would take me on, he said, on condition that I put aside all of my wonderful ideas (he accused me of being a dilettante) and concentrate, for the whole summer, on just one thing. Boy that was a lesson. Wouldn't it be good, he seemed to suggest, if I took all that creative mayhem, and tried to discover something more enduring. That lesson has stayed with me—the value of narrowing a focus, and giving it time.

∿

I visited Japan, and travelled to see the Golden Temple. I was struck by the beauty of the landscape, and the delicacy of the culture. Everything seemed considered and formalised; pottery, tea ceremonies, temple architecture, brush painting, even the wrapping of a gift in a department store were elevated and formalised. But within the formal choreographed settings I discovered moments of fantastic spontaneous communal life, orchestrated by the slightest architecture.

I took a trip to the mountains and went to visit some *onsen*, hotsprings. A little village was mostly comprised of exquisite inns amongst the trees and rocks that had hot sulphurous baths between the buildings. Here Japanese couples, old and young, stripped off and hung out together, naked up in the woods, and then clopped about the village in their slippers and robes. Later, back in the city, I ate at a street noodle stall, that was nothing more than curtains hanging around a frame. From the outside I saw trousered people, truncated at the waist, and steam rising up above. Once inside simple food was prepared with precision; plenty of saki was going down. How wonderful to be in the middle of a crowded street, visible from the waist down, and feel so private!

I learned the value of surprise, of turning an opportunity into an event, and the idea of orchestration in architecture.

∿

Arriving at Kettle's Yard as a student I'm not sure I appreciated what it would, in time, come to mean for me. Hungry as I was for experience of the great wide world I missed what it had to offer. Yet something kept pulling me back, returning each time not only to see what latest show was on, but to wander through the house. I wouldn't have done so, I'm sure, for the collection. I returned, I think, to be reminded what life *could* be about, and how architecture can orchestrate these possibilities. Here I was able to think about these things without 'style' interfering. Kettle's Yard stripped away the history of '-isms' and Movements; here I could have a personal relationship with the work, and view it for pleasure rather than for the pursuit of knowledge. It made me think that I too could collect objects that will give meaning and provoke wonder.

The balance between a domestic and formal setting is artful. The half-space between the two buildings is not a home, but not a gallery either. It's an eerie perhaps, a platform, maybe a den. It's a place to drink mint tea in glasses or drink red wine deep into the night. The Leslie Martin addition is certainly not a home, but again the boundaries are blurred. It's a conversation pit, a library, a gallery, a dug-out cave far from the streets outside. It feels like it would be right with about 40 people, maybe in Kaftans, certainly looking for something new.

After a visit to the house I often come away thinking that many things are possible, as long as I have the will to challenge the way things are, and imagine how they could be. It challenges convention, it eschews pomposity, it sees curiosity as a virtue. And it reminds me that what is of more value than all the -isms of Art and Movements of Architecture, is to spend one summer, looking at just one thing.

SUSAN WATSON

A Bowl by Lucie Rie

It's there. A curve of opaque light. Pure form.
The subtlety of not quite white. It's clear
that emphasis has been erased in making.

The pressure of the hand, the marks of making,
the language and the stories that inform
the rhythm of its shape, spin clear

away. A rim that dips and climbs and forms
a perfect imperfection in its making.
Perched on a graceful foot, the light curve clear.

Making form light, single and clear and there.

Jeremy Hooker

On Looking into *A Way of Life*

'... in a world rocked by greed, misunderstanding and fear, with
the imminence of collapse into unbelievable horrors, it is still
possible and justifiable to find important the exact placing of
two pebbles.'

— Jim Ede

in and out of the paintings
          in and out of the rooms
the way of the maker leads
round and round
                    pebble
by pebble
shell by shell

          circling
          tracing with the mind's fingers
grain of wood
bowl & jug
fisherman's glass ball

shadow takes hold among the things
light plays silent notes

'the joy of opening windows'
the joy of closing them
          the maker's face
reflected in painted glass

outside – the sea

still energy
from savaged hands
'something of transparent peace'

instant made to last

feather-light
on massive swell
the boat
          this man's life
risen in his mind
bedded in his flesh

come to rest
where the spirit's hand moves
round and round

in living space
                in and out

JACOB POLLEY

Stones on a Windowsill

These nine stones have come to a halt
though time has not—has it not?—stopped.
The sea is a voice and a mouth.

Time has not stopped, though these nine stones
have been brought to this windowsill,
out of the sea, which is a clock

and a voice and a mouth.
They have come to stand, not
for nine full stops, but for silence.

John Kinsella

Henri Gaudier-Brzeska and Me

SOMEBODY ASKED ME about 'character' today. What's in a character? they asked. How would I know? I replied. I could see they'd written me over, written me out, written me off . . . I was a character to them and this was irony.

I am looking back through the window, into where I was this afternoon. Where I'd inculcated myself among the browsers, the know-alls, the food-lovers. They eat aesthetics. There were some school kids among them, giggling. When are we going to start making the movie? one of them asked. It's not a movie, another responded. One of the boys rubbed a sculpture and a girl rolled her tongue over her lips. Sex, I thought, is mostly an act of boredom.

All this still action in stone. They say he died when he was only twenty-three, but it being the Great War, twenty-three wasn't such a young age. He sculpted plenty and he is still ripe, ripe for plucking.

I am looking back through the window, into where I am now between sculptures. I am in my own 'their' space, cleaning away the dust, the specks of DNA, the cobwebs. One doesn't completely dissolve the presence of DNA—one damages it. Lights in a gallery are never too bright. The cleaning fluids . . .

It's such a dangerous corner—just down from here. Traffic with nowhere to go—a carpark, through the bollards if you're a cab or have got an electronic zapper . . . or a bus . . . —students and tourists and townspeople . . . all different . . . squeezed into the medieval. Over the river.

And up the hill, the foundations, the old castle place with its high weeds and semi-marketable resolve. Further down, the Isaac Newton. Sitting at the bus-stop opposite with a girl-friend, I chucked up after a Friday night drinking with the others. I got done by a student who thought all his Christmases had come at once. They had. I'd seen him down at the Henri Gaudier-Brzeska, trying to work out whether it was cooler to look wealthy or poor. He had the jacket and glasses and accent to turn both tricks.

I am looking back through the window, into where I will be tomorrow evening when they've all gone home. Some kind of speech on the cusp of evening, drinks, chitter-chatter. Those . . . these . . . this large plate-glass window. It's not only light that makes reflections, it's how you look, how long you look. I see myself at all ages, in all circumstances. Mainly I am alone, bent over, cleaning floors, fighting dust and the glances of statues that have no real faces. The failure of all art if writ in the eyes. The lack of real eyes.

1891–1915. It's not long, not long really. I'm not far off that. Not really. I heard one boffin say that he studied the Chinese. I wondered. In the family, I am told my great-great-grandmother was Chinese. Me? I am a Londoner trans-planted to Cambridge. I am 'exotic' here too. It's only okay if you're a student or a teacher. Looking back through the window, I see them form shapes with their mouths, enclosing me in their kisses. I bend and swish the surfaces. I wear nothing close-fitting. I am their ideogram, next to the sculptures they know so much about, they pass by again and again, saying they can't get enough. I am, I guess, a character.

I am looking back through the window, into where I was this afternoon. Just a part of the crowd. An art-lover taking an interest. Crossing the cultural space, the hot zone. I wore heels and a short skirt as if they mattered, as if they were part of a performance I wasn't attending. They walked separately, and I looked closely at the statues . . . the sculptures. I stand corrected.

Migrations

Late winter afternoon;
the light shrunk to long shadows
hunched beneath the barn

and a scribble of crows
wheeling in the tractors' wake
above the furrowed fields.

There is such loneliness
among this clot of ragged wings
where something is stirring in the blood,

a gathering disquiet, as the raucous
cries stain the wind black as ink.
December dusk

and the grey sky lies in tatters
along the hedgerows.
Some deep imperative

compels this tribal gathering,
this restless leaving;
the tilting of a hundred tiny

hearts, each pointing
like the needles of a compass
towards a dream of home.

Tamar Yoseloff

The Venetian Mirror

*When I first hung it in our bedroom we could not sleep all night,
it was like having the moon for company, so bright it shone*
— Jim Ede

1.

Silver has its day, recedes
to reveal the surface beneath

gone black—
its own Dorian moment.

It reflects back what we have
not been able to understand,

an abundance lost, just hinted
in the etched leaves, tendrils lacing

the frame. What's inside is
rust, a pox on a lovely face,

still we trade its dimensions
for our own: dumbstruck, vain.

2.

The basilica behind a slick
of rain, gold diminished

to dun. The colour of nothing.
The bulk of it jagged

on the darkening sky.
The end of day, odic light

illuminates a shrivelled rose;
all the sadness we contain

in this drop of rain, its
crystallised gloom.

3.

The ghost hulk of the palazzo
leans into the canal. Narcissus crazed.

Tarnished jewels, pink marble
dulled to flesh. Shiver of a ballroom

out of season, sliver of broken
glass, the first glistening of frost,

as the campana strikes,
mourns itself in echo.

LAWRENCE SAIL

The Challenge

FROM THE OUTSET, it might be the corollary of a dream, one very like a fairytale. You arrive at a house that has something secretive about it, though it is impossible to say exactly in what way. It doesn't appear to be made of gingerbread. There is no sign of a bottle standing on a table, filled with a potion which might make you taller or smaller. To the right of the closed door, there is simply a bell-rope to be pulled. And, as you will know when you return for further visits, which is very likely to be the case, you have only to ring, and after a short pause someone always appears to let you in.

As with Dr Who's Tardis, what you might have comprehended from the exterior as you approached bears no relation to the nature or dimensions of the inside. You find yourself not in a space, or even a series of spaces, so much as an interspace. How could you define it? Hardly by its name: 'Kettle's Yard' conceals the nature and purposes of the house in the way that some poem titles decline to tell the reader what the poem is about. You can sketch the house's character roughly with negatives or partial truths, without being much the wiser. As Jim Ede said, whose house this was, it is not a museum. What museum is as free of labels and explicatory text as this place? Nor is it, quite, a gallery. How many galleries are adorned with fresh flowers in almost every room, or hang their pictures in such intimate settings as a bathroom or lavatory? Nor is it simply the evidence of one man's taste but rather, according to the man himself, 'a continuing way of life'. He also wanted the house to be more than a reflection of 'the taste of a given period'. On one level its interest is of course just that, yet the advent of Kettle Yard's fiftieth year, like its continuance beyond the lifetime of its founder, appears to prove him right: the interspace is temporal as well as spatial. And this impression is heightened by the way in which successive visits bring recognition and growing familiarity but also, always, objects and juxtapositions noticed properly for the first time. It is a bit like walking into that nexus of the moment and timelessness embodied in Eliot's *Four Quartets*.

The house easily defeats attempts at adequate description, if only because it is so easy to omit one or other essential component of its character. Perhaps there is something oneiric about this, too: nothing here is dissociated, or subject to a change of tense, not even the most secretive part of the house, the attic, with its warm gloaming like a shed in summer and, even though it is under the roof, also the deep-down sense of being somewhere below deck in an old wooden ship. Everything is conjoined in a totality, in associations of texture and light. Within this integrity, there is also the honouring of each singular object, the quiddity of each constituent part: yet nothing is roped off, or made into a precinct. Perhaps most unusually of all, though the lives of the artists whose pictures and sculptures and books make up the ensemble bear witness to their share of human struggle and sadness, there is nothing elegiac in the atmosphere. In the same way, the empty chairs, the china no longer used, the divan bed unrumpled—all are free of ghosts, while keeping somehow a sense of the actual and the particular that no museum-piece can ever quite retain. In many ways being here feels much more like being out of doors than in a confined interior: the affinities are with uncluttered landscapes, with objects intensified by the natural light coming and going around them, with the Protean moods of the sea.

In the house you wander as you choose. You could be at a loss, though there are benign guardians who will point you in the right direction, or give information if you require it. They are at their best when they hover silently, available but not insistent. There is so much to take in, so much that claims you—the grain of wood, the shapes and patterns of pebbles arranged in a coil of punctuation, the polished energy of sculpted stone, Alfred Wallis's sailing boats and trawlers pitching in seas where the submerged fish loom like lost souls, the hieratic obliquities of David Jones's multi-layered paintings, Henri Gaudier-Brzeska's bird swallowing a fish, Ben Nicholson's explorations of space and light. And everywhere those vases of flowers, never overblown, entirely without ostentation, more like posies gathered on an afternoon walk than anything more formal.

You find your way at your own pace, from small ground floor rooms up a narrow stair to a roomier first floor: then up to and down from the attic, before discovering the broader spaces of the extension. In doing so, you undertake a progress that might be said to mirror what Robert Frost wrote about the figure a poem should make—one that begins with delight and ends in wisdom. But you only become aware of this as you leave Kettle's Yard, when you look out across the threshold, or later when you think back to your visit. You begin to see how much perception depends on context. What you have taken home with you is not just what Jim Ede called 'a continuity of enjoyment', but the notion of continuity in itself. It is as if, having experienced an ideogram of a space in which art and nature might co-exist on equal terms, you are challenged now to seek expressions of its name in the world outside.

ELAINE FEINSTEIN

Kettle's Yard

It was happiness they painted, Renoir and Monet:
    the delicate landscape of Chatou,
a boy running through a golden field of grass,
      with dabs of red poppies, blobs of flurried blue.

Kettle's Yard is sober in my memory:
      quiet space and light on bare wood,
stone we could touch, a sculptured fish:
        contentment, much needed in a cold city.

SARAH SKINNER

The House

It is the light that lives here now,
plays along the broken lines and glass,
leans against the objects on the floor,
shadows of the fragile and the small,
at rest. The figure bent beneath the stairs
born of flame, light bulbs in a cage,
the Beijing puppet, keeping watch
across an oiled sea.

I feel its weight, its glue that holds
each table leg, each chosen stone
each sketch of ships that fly
each floating face and staring eye;
the cherished and the broken things
of people gone away, that nestle
folded close inside these walls;
the cooling carcass of a sunlit day.

Wartime Aubade

I hear them before I see them
Their song as if music was about to run out

Rapid twitters mingle with lazy burbles
Instruments warm up in pattern and rhythm

So light from the east comes out slow
Rising from an underwater dark

Birdsong pulls the worm from this morning
Herds last night deep among trees

The world's first truck crests Brush Mountain
Dragging its parachute engine organ

Stop me before I run away with myself
To join an army of beaks and feathers

A light brigade pouring over the horizon
A dark enemy driven into the eaves

Rod Mengham

The Real Avant-Garde

I FIRST WALKED into Kettle's Yard shortly after arrival in Cambridge in 1973. I had come to study English and to try to write. For me—as for anyone concerned with experimental art—the house by the church gave spatial form to an historical problem. You could say it enshrined the paradox of the twentieth century avant-gardes: the pursuit of new forms, the discovery of organizing principles specific to the medium, and the vexed question of how these formalist goals relate to the society that has produced them. In Kettle's Yard, the question of how we actually live with experimental art was given practical form—and a very English character— in Jim Ede's arrangements, but the full scope of the question has been addressed and re-addressed in a series of temporary exhibitions. To my mind, the value of these exhibitions was epitomized in the Polish Constructivism show of 1984. This was typically far-sighted, bringing Polish Constructivist paintings, sculptures and publications to Britain for the first time, and typically over-arching, exhibition and catalogue together encapsulating an entire history of debate around issues echoed in the more familiar wrangles of western art movements.

Polish Constructivism between the mid-1920s and the late 1930s was essentially a series of arguments about the relationship between art and twentieth century production processes. There were three overlapping phases, each associated with different artistic groupings and group publications. The first, *Blok*, was the earliest and most short-lived, initiated in 1924 and succeeded in 1926 by *Praesens*, which lasted until 1939, despite a major change of direction and of personnel. Both of these movements involved collaboration and rivalry between artists and architects. The distinguishing feature of the third phase, which led to the formation of a group calling itself *a.r.*, was a series of joint projects involving both artists and writers. The initial letters *a.r.* stood alternatively for *awangarda rzeczywista* [the real avant-garde] and for *arstysci rewolucyjni* [revolutionary artists]. The obvious protagonist in each of these three scenarios was Wladyslaw Strzeminski, the most radical formalist in the history of Polish Constructivist painting, and the busiest controversialist. The reason *Blok* was so short-lived was intransigence on the part of both Strzeminski and Mieczyslaw Szczuka, who clashed over the theoretical subordination of art to questions of social utility. Szczuka wished to place art at the service of town- planning and industrial design, while Strzeminski believed in its independence from existing forms of urbanism as the basis for imagining entirely different social structures in the future. *Praesens* started harmoniously with the idea of promoting collaborations between artists and architects, seizing opportunities to impose abstract painted designs on existing buildings, and to interpose abstract sculptures in the spaces between buildings. However, after three years, Strzeminski left the group, together with the painter Henryk Stazewski and the sculptor Katarzyna Kobro, convinced of the need to replace these partial measures with a unified programme of urban design, where the emphasis was on the composition of the entire architectural environment according to the same principles. During the 1930s, Strzeminski pursued the goals of *a.r.* through the much narrower focus of typographical design, with remarkable results. His settings of the poems of Julian Przybos regarded the entire page as a unified field in which the various interrelated elements were of equal significance. By these means, the visual structure could be equal in importance to the aural structure.

After seeing the relevant works in the Kettle's Yard exhibition, I was offered a job soon afterwards that would put them close to the centre of my life for the next three years. In October 1984, I went to a Readership at the University of Lodz in Poland. Lodz is home to many things: the site of the second largest Jewish ghetto; the Polish film school; an extraordinarily unified nineteenth century archtectural heritage; the Museum of Modern Art. The latter was the source of practically all the works in the Kettle's Yard Exhibition. Here they made sense not only in the context of the history of the European avant-gardes, but in terms of local buildings, murals, applied art of various kinds, and in their influence on the stubborn formalism of post-war experiments in various media, particularly film. Strzeminski had taught in local schools and the results were widespread, affecting the practice of various crafts, especially textiles. If the official art of the communist era was socialist realism, it seemed that Constructivist principles were more immanent, less declamatory but more pervasive, less aggressive but more tenacious. I was impressed by the extent to which radical abstraction could be deployed as effective resistance to a dominant ideology. It deepened my respect for Strzeminski, for the consistency and coherence of his practice, and my curiosity about, and acclimatization to his work led to cooperation with Jozef Robakowski and Jarek Jedlinski, whose film about the painter appeared in 1993. I prepared the text for the English version of this, and provided the voice-over for the soundtrack. But although Strzeminski had been the driving force behind the conceptual integrity of Polish Constructivism, the most beguiling objects that it ever produced were the sculptures of Kobro, which I had seen for the first time in Castle Street. Over three years, I got to know them well and to appreciate the scope of Kobro's remark 'sculpture is a part of the space around it'. The positioning of the work, physically, socially, culturally, was an unignorable element in its reception. When the Polish art collective *fabs* asked me in 2000 for a statement of compositional practice, I began with Kobro's dictum, believing that it could reflect my sense of how I wanted the poetic text to relate to the different languages that surround it. But the debt was acknowledged in more suitable form in 1998, when the Museum of Modern Art published my poetic sequence 'Kobro' to coincide with a major retrospective exhibition there.

Part of the debt is owing to Kettle's Yard for introducing me to all of this. The point is not the coincidence of those works being exhibited in the very year that I was contemplating a move to Poland. The point is that Kettle's Yard is the kind of space in which those kinds of works will be shown. If the idea that sculpture is a part of the space around it is not actually inscribed on the lintel, it is implied equally by the dispositions of the house and by the exhibition programme of the gallery space. It is an idea whose true scope should never be underestimated.

SUE HUBBARD

New Year

Whited-out morning,
every movement erased
in this silvery vacancy,

nothing has form,
all is shift and flux
and the motions of mind

have nothing
to hang onto
here in this milky mist

where the only black
thing is a crow pecking
bleached rib bones

half buried in the mud.
Will the next hour look
like this, tomorrow

like today or will I wake
and from my small
window or open door

see the glittering cadences
of ocean, its tentative tracery
of gold fragile as breath

written on the waves like prayers
and the islands rising
in the January dawn with new meaning?

ALI SMITH

Seven Visits to Kettle's Yard

SUMMER 2007

I RING THE bell of the house, sign in and go straight upstairs.
The house is full, as usual, of happy-looking visitors. You can
tell the new from the old. The new ones wander about in a
wide-eyed exclamatory ecstasy of disbelief. The ones who're
returning either wander through the house with the kind of
pride that means they think it belongs to them, or, if they're
with someone, make straight for their favourite places and
artefacts, saying things like Come and see! or Wait till you see
it! In each of the rooms there's a polite and friendly—I'm
trying to think of the right word, warden? watcher? keeper?
—I mean the kind people who keep an eye on the art and
help the visitors with information, I meet one of these ladies
on the way upstairs and as I pass her I say, The Gaudier-
Brzeska room's still in the loft, isn't it? (I say it rhetorically,
really, because I know the room'll still be there, of course it'll
still be there, and partly because I'm one of those returning
visitors proud to be going back to something I already know
and love and keen to let others know that's what I am.) Yes it
is, she says, and then she adds, You know, it's the one room
I felt least comfortable about in the whole house in the first
little while of my working here. No, I say, it's not comforting,
is it, it's the opposite of comforting, it's properly modern in
its brittleness and its energy, it'll never date. Exactly, she says,
and I go off up the stairs of this most comforting house to the
unsettling nature of things sprung just under its roof, like a

76

trap for a wild creature, a room full of exactly that uncom-
forting wildness Gaudier-Brzeska catches in the jaw of the
fox, or the arrogant point of the little bearded jaw on the
Head of Ezra Pound, or the triangular, genital nothing-but-
mouth on the girl whose whole face is a joyful modernist
double-entendre. I'm there for about ten minutes, thinking
about the title of one of the most naturalist of the works,
Grace and Speed, the careful, naturalist rendition of the
wing of a big bird of prey, when I notice for the first time, in
a small picture of a line-up of tenement buildings at the
other end of the room, an unexpected streak of bright blue
running right through the picture's centre.

SUMMER 2006

I AM VISITING beautiful Farley Farm, in Sussex, where Lee
Miller and Roland Penrose lived. It's not far from Charleston,
where the Woolfs and the Bells made their home outside
London. I've visited both houses, both houses have been very
welcoming indeed and have given us, in one instance, an
organised tour, and in the other a private visit. In both cases
it feels like a real privilege. Both remind me of somewhere,
but for the moment, in the dining room of Farley Farm,
with its long wooden table in front of me, I can't think quite
where. Why do I keep wanting to sit on the chairs we're not
really meant to sit on? Why do I long to lift that book off the
shelf and have a look at it? Why do I expect that table in
front of me to be covered in books there for the looking at?
What rare place am I imagining where that level of intimacy
with a building like this is possible, where a visit has become

77

something else, a little different, unexpected, a kind of democratic? That place doesn't exist. I'm making it up, surely.

Spring 1986

I AM A new postgraduate student in a city whose rich beauty is still shocking to me, and whose economic richness is too. I've arrived in Cambridge from doing two degrees at a Scottish university, and I've come with all my precepts intact. I've never seen a city where the sheen of education is also somehow connected to the sheens of social hierarchy and money. I've been here six months or so, and I'm finding the sheen of it all a bit blinding. One winter's afternoon I visit a local art gallery, because an Irish girl, an undergraduate at one of the other colleges, and one of the few people I've met here who immediately recognised the sense of outsider that's clearly now sheening me, tells me I'll like it there. So I go, and what I will remember most clearly from this first visit, right there alongside all the astonishing art, is that more than a gallery it's a house, and more than a house it's a home. Next I will remember the light switches, and how they're made so that you can see, directly, how power works. Then there's the way the windows gather the town into the house, reconcile opposites like insider and outsider, give nature to art and give art to the trees and the pointed spire of the old church, revealing this house's tradition, an alternative art tradition, one of openness. It's no surprise, afterwards, when I hear that Jim Ede has strong links to Scotland. The real surprise to me, a passionate student of modernism at the time, is that this first afternoon, I find myself sitting in a comfortable old armchair in a house that feels like

78

someone's home, with a first edition of a T.S. Eliot poem there in my hands.

I AM DOWNSTAIRS in the large room when I see for the first time, round the corner on a narrow jut of wall, a Gabo picture I've somehow managed never to see before. It is blue and starry, like an imaginary sky, and has a curve of line in it making a dimensional shape out of what looks like thin air. Out of what seems near-nothing it opens into a revelation of space. It is like this house itself, whose narrow staircases open into light, into unexpected space after unexpected space, into yet more to see when you think you've seen it all.

THE BEAUTIFUL PIECE of sculpture on top of the piano, a piece of work whose rhythm is made of light and line and whose uniting of heaviness and lightness mirrors both the place it usually sits and the function of the instrument, has been moved. The grand piano, famous for being matt in surface finish, has its top open. The room is full of people. We get a very good seat, on one of the mattress-like cushions along the long wall, a good place because not only do we have a clear view of Jayne Parker's film work, we are also so close to Katharina Wolpe, there at the piano, that we can see the notes on the music she is reading, and the little hesitation of her hand as she senses the correct jagged rhythm. Wolpe is here to play some of the pieces her father composed and to be a live presence at Parker's extraordinary films of her performances. It is a uniting of artists that fills the house with the disciplined interplay of light and dark that is at the core of the music, the films and Wolpe's own life and difficult art. The final film ends, the music crashes to an end, there's a stunned moment of silence, then the audience roars appreciation. One more time this house has allowed for the crossing of borders between genres that lets art be that much more alive.

SPRING 1988

I HAVE A brand new lover, which makes me a brand new lover myself. Nearly twenty years after this particular spring, when I tell her I'm writing this piece, she'll laugh and describe to me how I took her to the house and made straight for the Gaudier-Brzeska dachshund on the stairs. Wait till you see the dog on the stairs. Wait till you see the glass thing that makes the plants and the light come together. Wait till you see the picture that's all blacks, of a moon or a sun in a black landscape, and the way the church picture on the far wall echoes the shape of the house roof. Now come and see the piano, it's matt so its surface won't reflect light. They did it specially. Wait till you see the fawn. Come and see the wrestlers.

Autumn 1992

I AM BACK living in Cambridge again, after a couple of years away. For a couple of years I've been telling people elsewhere how the nature of the house is an inspiration when it comes to how to have a home and how to treat art, both; how it demonstrates that the home is an art, and how it demonstrates that art can be a home. Now that I'm back living here again, one of the first things I do is visit.

Any Time You Like
(from 2.00 p.m. to 4.00 p.m. excluding Mondays)

THERE IS AN unexpected Miró picture just round the corner in the first downstairs room you come into after you've signed the book. The Gaudier-Brzeska collection is crouched, waiting, in the loft. There's a table you can sit at, for hours if you want, and read. There's a sense, as you pass through the house, of being inside some kind of miraculous structure that keeps on opening up, more and more. There's a sense that its art is always giving, is neverending. There's even a sense in which you'll enjoy looking at the tap or the sinks or the toilet in the little back room. This is what Kettle's Yard does to the senses. It's a place that makes everything more. There's an old wooden wedge attached to a piece of cord at the right hand side of the outside door, and what you do is you take it in your hand and you pull it, which makes a bell ring inside, then they open the door and in you go.

SHARON MORRIS

Kettle's Yard House

THE VIEW

A cormorant and two gulls in flight
through a flux of light and air

that occludes the horizon, except
for a cull of marks, a sooty squall

distinct from the shiny sea. *Seascape
from a Terrace* by David Jones.

As in his *Manawydan's Glass Door*,
closed against sorrow and loss,

all is translucent, a passage from myth
into time. Here, out of the window

you can see a pear tree in fruit, a bay
of rosemary, flag irises and thistles.

Seascape from a Terrace, David Jones,1929,
Manawydan's Glass Door, David Jones, 1931,
(collection of Arthur Giardelli).

THE TREE

Its roots in earth, flowering in heaven,
Yggdrasil, axis of the world, tree as Cross,

Cross as tree, stands at Calvary between
the tree of the good thief and the tree of power.

Chestnut, pine and fir, seen from the window
of David Jones' nursing home, transfigured

in this drawing that flows from forest floor
to the uppermost branch and sparse leaf —

a Paschal Candle shot with five nails,
five wounds. A pelican feeds its young.

Ponies standing in for the Roman cavalry
race through rolling hills towards the collapse

of Empire. A winged female figure guards
the sacred well and its rushing stream.

The tree extends across both riverbanks,
its leaves for the healing of nations.

Vexilla Regis, David Jones, 1948.

WORD MADE FLESH

Maybe it's Ede's game to
hang David Jones's inscription
Quia per Incarnati directly
above William Scott's
Message Obscure I; otherwise
why hang these enigmatic hooves
of black print (signs, indexes,
traces of a cloven animal)
beneath Roman lettering
(utterances of text in a script
for chiselled stone) here,
if not as creation ex nihilo?

Quia per Incarnati by David Jones, 1953.
Message Obscure I, William Scott, 1965.

BIRD SWALLOWING A FISH

A single bed under the sloping attic roof
offers a place to think, to take a leap, a plié,
with the grace and speed of an eagle's wing —

Gaudier's sinuous line slides through itself,
knotting into eagle, monkey, fox, hen,
and cat that glares and jumps out of the frame.

Pound, the grandfather of modernism,
ABC, looks down over the avant-garde,
and is swallowed with the fish by the bird.

> *Grace and Speed* or *The Golden Eagle's Wing*, 1908,
> *Ezra Pound*, 1914,
> *Bird Swallowing a Fish*, Henri Gaudier-Brzeska, 1914.

CHORA

Flora in Calix-Light, three glass
chalices of light and flowers—

wine-red carnations and ears of corn,
blue cornflowers and thorny-stemmed

roses, shedding petals of blood.
Marks, as if by chance, defining

space as substance—pencil lines
and fleeting brushstrokes coalesce

into stillness. The lock and catch
of the window anchoring the world

that could swing wide open. His hand
pressed between glass and paper.

Flora in Calix-Light, David Jones, 1950.

EMPTINESS

Etana, Giardino a Mezzogiorno, Pietra,
black and white sheets of torn paper,
matter disintegrating into
nothingness.

On the dresser
stands an empty bowl.
Above, a high shelf of white plates,
and sitting in the corner cupboard, Buddha.

> *Etana, Giardino a Mezzogiorno*, Pietra, Italo Valenti, 1964.
> *Bowl, The Wave*, Lucie Rie, 1971.
> Buddha, Mandalay, 18th century.

EXTENSION

Mermaid of white marble, her face
gazing upwards, her fish-tail flat
as a flipper.

Three black sails, three obelisks
of black stone leaning into each other,
Three Personages.

Maria Carmi as the Madonna,
Maria Carmi as mountain.

Mermaid, 1912–13 by Henri Gaudier-Brzeska.
Three Personages, Barbara Hepworth, 1965.
Maria Carmi as the Madonna, 1912.

Ben Nicholson's *Musical Instruments*,
two guitars painted in sombre colours,
and *Wrestlers*, by Gaudier-Brzeska,
a relief showing two men locked together,
hang either side of the Steinway.

Placed on the closed lid, *Construction in Space*
by Naum Gabo: two perspex wings intersect,
strung with nylon filaments, held taut
in a tight paradox of topology,
a cross opening out into the swift curves
of a bird in flight, heartstrings
to be plucked like a lyre, a dualism of
matter and light, flickering like a flame, Orpheus
made visible in that high-pitched frequency.

I heard Katharina Wolpe play her father's music
on this piano, *Stationary Music*, tireless, ceaseless
yet, achingly beautiful, this music without
development or progress, and without respite,
the meaning of the word 'perseverate' —
to repeat and never be done with.

Musical Instruments, Ben Nicholson, 1933.
Wrestlers relief, Henri Gaudier-Brzeska, 1914.
Construction in Space, Naum Gabo, 1962.
Performance of Stefan Wolpe's *Stationary Music*, 2006.

SENSETIVO

In the first account of the myth,
'Orpheus and Euridyce',
Orpheus never made that fatal mistake,
looking back over his shoulder
to check if she is following him out of hell,
his music successfully charms the dead
and he brings back his love to life.

I think of this, listening to Anton
playing Bussotti's *Sensetivo*,
as he grapples with the cello, scratching
at wood, plucking strings, tapping
broken rhythms, scoring his nails
into the polished surface,
his concentration, absolute, haptic.

In front of him stands Rodin's *Eve*,
her arms crossed over her body,
one hand emerging from bronze
as if still clay, her other hand
raised to shield her face: she drops
her gaze and shies away from him.

Sensetivo, Sylvano Bussotti, 1959,
Performed by Anton Lukoszevieze
for a film by Jayne Parker, 2007.
Eve, Rodin, 1881 (Southampton City Gallery).

90

THE BECHSTEIN ROOM

Brought to rest on the lid
of the closed piano, a teardrop
cast in black cement from

a child's head carved out of marble,
Prometheus. No eyelids
or lips, the nose a subtle line,

a recess under the brow,
ovoid head balanced on his ear
as if listening to Orpheus,

whose music distracted the eagle
pecking at Prometheus's liver
and stopped that eternal torment.

Prometheus, Constantin Brancusi, 1912.

DAVID HARE

Amy's View of Kettle's Yard

THERE'S NO DOUBT that in the mind of the Cambridge undergraduate in 1965, music, politics, drama and literature had a great deal more to offer than the visual arts. With Tate Bankside opening in the year 2000 and the lives of painters now regularly eulogised in the Sunday papers, it's almost impossible to recapture the spirit of a time when you could call yourself educated and yet have no idea of what was happening in the world of modern art.

I think of myself as a typical undergraduate of the period. I came to study at Jesus College, Cambridge already well versed in Sartre, Rosa Luxemburg and D.H. Lawrence and yet without the slightest idea of who Brancusi was, or where a Vorticist might part company from a Surrealist. There was, admittedly, a terrific college collection from which undergraduates were allowed to borrow on a termly basis for a peppercorn deposit. But when I placed a shining Barbara Hepworth maquette on my mock-Tudor-ugly desk in the Tudor-ugly room where I worked, then it was probably with the feeling that I had thereby got the whole business of feeding my eyes conveniently out of the way.

It was just luck, then, that a friend called Roger Vellacott wearied of whatever subject he was reading, and decided instead to switch to Fine Art. Pretty soon after, Roger came back to the rest of us with news of an eccentric collector, just beyond Magdalene, who was willing, every afternoon, to open his house to whoever wanted to visit. The idea sounded intriguing. I remember stringing along, more with the idea of seeing who such a weird person might be than with any particular intention of looking at what was on his walls. Curiosity, however, is the only true essential of aesthetics—without curiosity you have nothing, in life or in art—and the person, it turned out, was Jim Ede.

From this distance, you can only speculate how this mannerly English gentleman would have reacted to the plentiful crowds who presently flow through Kettle's Yard, and who now treat its existence as an artistic given. It's become a rare example of something which is no less beautiful for being bigger. But in those days, there were certainly long afternoons when I was alone, or in the company of only one or two friends. It wasn't any particular work of art or artefact which drew me—though Gaudier, of course, dominated the rooms as he did Jim's conversation. More, it was the feeling, completely new to me, that modernity could be calming, and that the place where you lived could embody the idea of who you were as a person.

The calm was both a surprise and a paradox. We had all so taken it for granted that revolution was born in turbulence that it was amazing to be introduced to a progressive group of artists who nevertheless possessed some inner poise or balance. Critics of Kettle's Yard—if they exist—would no doubt say that its domesticity is an expression of the limitations of British, or British-influenced, art. But that's not how I saw it then. Nor now. In the screaming herringbone and tie-dye of the sixties, the white spaces of Kettle's Yard seemed strikingly continental in their sense of freedom and their emphasis on refining your vision. For the three years I remained at Cambridge, time spent with Jim's collection was not just an inspiring antidote to the far more tendentious education I was receiving from my official teachers. It also provided welcome moments of lucidity and rest.

In 1998, when I wrote *Amy's View*, I led the great theatrical designer Bob Crowley on his first visit to Kettle's Yard, because Jim's house so embodied the spirit of the fictional dead painter in whose home the action of the play takes place. Thanks to Judi Dench's exceptional performance as the painter's widow, the play enjoyed a popularity which propelled it first from the National Theatre to the West End, and then subsequently on to Broadway. Nothing amused me more about the experience of the play's transit than slipping quietly into the back of the auditorium on 48th Street and finding an audience of 1,200 Manhattan residents looking at a passable imitation of a Cambridge museum I had begun to visit 35 years previously.

Playwrights draw inspiration from odd places. It's confounding, how some random image suddenly becomes radioactively alive, and provides you with a source, a starting-point. I can't explain why the memory of Jim sitting with a rug over his knees somehow set me off thinking about a whole generation of unsung heroes—painters and sculptors—who went about their works with commitment but without ostentation. For me, Kettle's Yard will always remain a monument to virtue—both to the virtue of the collector and to that of the artists it represents. No puffing, no false pride. May it prosper as it deserves.

LAWRENCE SAIL

Edenic

Yet there are such places
of the outside-in
dream of order,
where every gift
of the light is more
than its parts and each
part remains whole in itself.

And here is one, conjured
by a tug on the bell-rope
—the locus of pigments
in bloom, stone's
coiled energy,
the irreducible
grain that runs through
worked and unworked wood.

In the mind's traverse which links
the maker's hand
and the viewer's eye,
or the distant shore
and this inland calm,
what is it that gives
each instance its weight,
the full glow of nature?

Just so, this little vase
of lilies of the valley
on a round table;
this cup worn
by usage; even
the book left splayed
at this or this page
by a reader who might return.

It is nothing less than retrieval,
the gift of attention
that slows the pulse
to proper health—
the material world
held to account
by the soul, and not found wanting.

List of Contributors

ALAN BENNETT's stage plays include *The Madness of George III*, *The Lady in the Van*, and most recently, *The History Boys*, which won three Olivier awards, a Critics' Circle Theatre Award and two Evening Standard Awards in the UK and six Tony awards on Broadway. A film adaptation was released in 2006. He has written numerous plays for television, including the series of monologues, *Talking Heads*. He is the author of two prose collections, *Writing Home* and *Untold Stories*. He is a frequent visitor to Kettle's Yard.

ANNE BERKELEY is one of The Joy of Six, with whom she has read at poetry festivals, in back rooms of pubs, and more than once in a large draughty tent. *The buoyancy aid and other poems* appeared from Flarestack in 1997, and a selection of poems was included in *Oxford Poets 2002* (Carcanet). Her first full collection is due from Salt in 2008.

MEREDITH BOWLES, AA Dipl RIBA, was educated at the University of Sheffield, the Royal College of Art and the Architectural Association, and is the current Chair of the Cambridge Association of Architects. Meredith has lectured widely and has been active in promoting sustainable design. Director of Mole Architects and Partner of studiomgm architects, he is the architect for the recently completed new building for the University of Cambridge Department of Architecture, and has been visiting Kettle's Yard since a student for restorative inspiration.

RICHARD BURNS's long and affectionate relationship with Kettle's Yard goes back to the 1970's, when he founded the first international Cambridge Poetry Festival (CPF); Kettle's Yard was the venue for several CPF exhibitions as well as numerous performances. He has been involved in various 'word-and-image' collaborations with artists, most recently with Paulo Gaspar Ferreira, Kip Gresham and Michael Judge. He has lived in Cambridge since 1969, published more than 20 poetry books and received numerous literary awards. His latest collection is *The Blue Butterfly* (Salt, 2006). Website: http://www.richardburns.eu/site/

MICHAEL BYWATER is a writer, critic and broadcaster. He read first medicine, then English, at Cambridge, spent many years on the staff of *Punch* magazine, and has been a columnist and contributor for many national newspapers. He has also written screenplays and computer games, and keeps himself honest by teaching a little Tragedy at Cambridge. He was writer-in-residence at Magdalene College in 2006.

His next book is *Like Brothers: On Men and Friendship*, to be published in 2008.

CLARE CROSSMAN moved to Cambridge from Cumbria in 2000. Her pamphlet collection *Landscapes* won the Redbeck Competition in 1996. Her work was included in *Take 5* (Shoestring Press, 2004) and Firewater Press Cambridge published *Going Back* in 2002. Some of her work has been set to music. Clare first went to Kettle's Yard in 2003 whilst studying the long poems of David Jones. The interiors of artists' houses are always a source of inspiration for her.

TONY CURTIS is Professor of Poetry at the University of Glamorgan where he leads the M.Phil. in Writing. His ninth collection *Crossing Over* has just appeared from Seren, as have two edited books on Wales and war in the twentieth century. He first fell in love with Kettle's Yard in the late 1980s and developed a serious affair with the place during his daughter's time at Clare College from 1995.

FRED D'AGUIAR lived and worked in Cambridge as a Judith E. Wilson Fellow in the late '80s . He visited Kettle's Yard tanked-up on the poetry he'd enjoyed from his work with Ken Edwards, Eric Mottram and Gillian Allnutt for their bravura anthology, *New British Poetry* (Paladin, 1988). The anthology's formal and philosophical innovations and inclusiveness shaped his poetry books, *British Subjects* (Bloodaxe, 1992), *Bill Of Rights* (Chatto, 1998) and his verse novel, *Bloodlines* (Vintage, 2000).

JANE DURAN was born in Cuba and brought up in the United States and Chile. Her collection *Breathe Now, Breathe* (Enitharmon, 1995) won the Forward Prize for Best First Collection. Enitharmon published her second collection, *Silences from the Spanish Civil War*, in 2002. Her third collection, *Coastal* (Enitharmon, 2005) received a PBS Recommendation. She received a Cholmondeley Award in 2005. In 1995 she gave a reading at Kettle's Yard together with Ruth Padel at an evening of poetry and music.

ELAINE FEINSTEIN was brought up in Leicester and educated at Newnham College, Cambridge, where she has lived as a poet, novelist and biographer since 1980. Her work has received many awards, including a Cholmondeley Award for Poetry, an Honorary D.Litt from the University of Leicester, and a Rockefeller Foundation Fellowship at Bellagio. She received a major Arts Council award for her new novel, *The Russian Jerusalem*, out in 2008. Her latest book of poems is *Talking to the Dead*. While living in Cambridge, she often visited Kettle's Yard.

JOHN GREENING (born 1954) has published a dozen collections, his latest, *Iceland Spar*, the result of a Society of Authors travel grant. *Falls*, to music by Paul Mottram, was premiered at the Wigmore Hall by the Dunedin Consort. He has won the Bridport and TLS prizes. He recently produced books on war poetry, Yeats, Hughes and Hardy. Having lived in Egypt and the USA, for many years now he has been within an X5 bus-ride of Kettle's Yard: a continual delight and welcome distraction from 'getting and spending'.

DAVID HARE is a playwright and screenwriter whose work includes *Plenty*, *Racing Demon*, *Skylight*, *Stuff Happens* and the film of *The Hours*. In the 1960s he studied at Cambridge University and relaxed at Kettle's Yard.

JEREMY HOOKER'S most recent publications are *The Cut of the Light: Poems 1965–2005* and *Upstate: A North American Journal*. He first visited Kettle's Yard in 1975 to see an exhibition of David Jones's paintings, during the first Cambridge International Poetry Festival, when he gave a lecture on Jones. Whenever in Cambridge, he visits Kettle's Yard, for the sake of the place itself, and because it contains work by some of his favourite artists.

SUE HUBBARD is twice winner of the London Writers competition, she was The Poetry Society's Public Art Poet responsible for London's largest public art poem at Waterloo. She has published two collections: *Everything Begins with the Skin* (Enitharmon, 1994) and *Ghost Station* (Salt, 2004) and her poems appeared in *Oxford Poets 2000*, Carcanet. Her first novel, *Depth of Field*, is published by Dewi Lewis. She writes on art for *The Independent* and *New Statesman* and wrote the Kettle's Yard catalogue essay on Rodin's Eve.

MARTHA KAPOS is the Assistant Poetry Editor of *Poetry London*. She won the Jerwood/Aldeburgh Prize for Best First Collection for *My Nights in Cupid's Palace* (Enitharmon 2003) which also received a PBS Special Commendation. Born in America, she came to London for a gap year following her Classics degree from Harvard, and never returned. It was while she was studying painting and art history at Chelsea School of Art that she first discovered the wonderful collection of pictures and objects at Kettle's Yard.

JOHN KINSELLA is a Fellow of Churchill College, Cambridge. He does the walk back from the centre of town to his rooms via Kettle's Yard. He is always looking through the front window of the main gallery, and occasionally wanders inside. He is a poet with a love of art.

ROD MENGHAM is Reader in Modern English Literature at the University of Cambridge, where he is also Curator of Works of Art at Jesus College. He is the author of books on Charles Dickens, Emily Brontë and Henry Green, and has edited collections of essays on contemporary fiction, violence and avant-garde art. *Unsung: New and Selected Poems* was published by Salt in 2001. He curated the biennial sculpture shows at Jesus College in 2003, 2005 and 2007, and has returned to Kettle's Yard innumerable times since his fist visit in 1973.

JOHN MOLE (born 1941) was a student at Magdalene College and a regular visitor to Kettle's Yard. After Cambridge he kept in close touch with Jim Ede, and more recently, on returning to Magdalene as poet in residence and as assistant director of the college's Literary Festival, he has made many further visits. His own apprentice pamphlet of verse can still be found in the house among books presented to Jim by poets and artists who have owed so much to him.

SHARON MORRIS studied fine art at the Slade School, where she currently teaches. She first visited Kettle's Yard as a student when she was became interested in the work of David Jones. In 2006 Anton Lukoszevieze, New Music Fellow at Kettle's Yard, invited her to read her poetry with a selection of Black Mountain School poems at a lunchtime-concert given by clarinettist Andrew Sparling. Her first collection, *False Spring*, was published by Enitharmon Press in 2007.

RUTH PADEL has published six collections, most recently *The Soho Leopard*, shortlisted for the T S Eliot Prize, and also non-fiction, including a recent book about reading modern poetry, *The Poem and the Journey*. In 2002 she did a reading and workshop tour for the British Council in Rangoon and Mandalay. She has taught Greek at Kings College, is a great great grandchild of Charles Darwin and lived in Cambridge from 1985–1990 when she often visited Kettle's Yard.

IAN PATTERSON is a writer, poet, translator, and former bookseller who now teaches English at Queens' College, Cambridge. His most recent books are *Guernica and Total War* (Profile, 2007) and *Time To Get Here: Selected Poems 1969–2002* (Salt 2003). He translated the final volume of Marcel Proust's *A la recherche du temps perdu* for Penguin (*Finding Time Again, Penguin*, 2003). He has been a fairly regular visitor to Kettle's Yard since 1966.

JACOB POLLEY was born in Carlisle, but spent 2005–07 in Cambridge, as a visiting Fellow at Trinity College. Kettle's Yard became somewhere he went, often with visiting friends or students, for a companionable wander and look-see. He grew to love the sense of arranged peace, and sharing that peace as he felt Kettle's Yard shared it with him. He has published two poetry collections with Picador, *The Brink* and *Little Gods*.

ANDREA PORTER knocked on Jim Ede's door in 1965, as an awkward teenage schoolgirl, and asked if he would show her round his home. It was the first time she realised that art and the word home could be spoken of in the same breath. She apologised for being nosy, and will always recall his answer. 'Nosiness' he reflected, 'is the key to any interest in the arts, encourage curiosity, it will stand you in good stead.' She is a member of the Cambridge-based poetry group, The Joy of Six.

LAWRENCE SAIL has published nine collections of poems, most recently *Eye-Baby* (Bloodaxe, 2006). He has compiled and edited a number of anthologies, including *First and Always: Poems for Great Ormond Street Children's Hospital* (Faber, 1988) and, with Kevin Crossley-Holland, *The New Exeter Book of Riddles* (Enitharmon, 1999) and *Light Unlocked* (Enitharmon, 2005). Enitharmon also published *Cross-currents*, a book of his essays, in 2005. Going to Kettle's Yard, then introducing it to students on the Madingley writing course he tutors each summer has been an abiding source of delight.

FIONA SAMPSON has published fifteen books, of which the most recent are *Common Prayer* (Carcanet, 2007), short-listed for the T.S. Eliot Prize, and a book of essays, *On Listening* (2007). She has received the Newdigate Prize and was short-listed for the 2006 Forward Prize for best single poem. She is Fellow in Performance and Creativity at the University of Warwick and Editor of *Poetry Review*; and contributes regularly to *The Guardian* and *Irish Times*.

SARAH SKINNER was raised in Johannesburg, South Africa, where she starting writing poetry at school, inspired by some of the Black and Afrikaans poetry that was emerging from there in the 80s. She won a prize for poetry at 15 and has been writing on and off ever since. Her parents met at Cambridge University and her poem, 'The House', was inspired by memories she had from visits to the campus as a child and by a recent visit to Kettle's Yard.

ALI SMITH was born in Inverness and lives in Cambridge. She has written four novels and three collections of short stories, the latest of which is *Girl Meets Boy* (Canongate, 2007).

ROBERT VAS DIAS is the author of seven poetry collections in the USA and UK, has edited literary journals and the anthology *Inside Outer Space* (NY: Doubleday), and is editor-publisher of Permanent Press. His new collection, *Leaping Down to Earth*, with images by Stephen Chambers and Tom Hammick, will be published in 2008. He conducted the Black Mountain Poetry & Poetics workshop for Kettle's Yard in 2006. He is a Tutor with The Poetry School in London and writes on book art and artists' books.

SUSAN WATSON was born in Derbyshire in 1958. She read English at Girton College and studied Creative Writing at the University of East Anglia. Although she discovered Kettle's Yard relatively recently, the house itself and the objects in it have become an important source of inspiration for her poems.

NEIL WENBORN is a full-time writer and a regular visitor to Kettle's Yard since his time as an undergraduate at Magdalene College in the 1970s. The author of biographies of Haydn, Stravinsky and Dvořák, and co-editor of the *History Today Companion to British History* and CUP's *Dictionary of Jewish–Christian Relations*, he was recently an organiser of the Magdalene Year in Literature Festival. A collection of his poetry, *Firedoors*, is published by Rockingham Press.

TAMAR YOSELOFF's third poetry collection, *Fetch*, was published by Salt in 2007, as was *Marks*, a collaboration with the artist Linda Karshan, which was published as both a limited edition book and pamphlet by Pratt Contemporary Art. She was Writer in Residence at Magdalene College in 2005, as part of their Year in Literature Festival, and during her stint there made Kettle's Yard her home away from home. She is currently working on her first novel and is the poetry editor of *Art World* magazine.

Acknowledgements

Extracts from 'Diaries: 2003' and 'Art, Architecture and Authors' © Alan Bennett. From *Untold Stories*, London: Faber & Faber / Profile Books 2005. Reprinted with the permission of the publisher.

'Fiddle Fish and Wave at Kettles Yard' © Clare Crosman, was first published in *Chapman* (Scotland) 108.

'After "The Island (with constant chaos)"' © Robert Vas Dias. From *Leaping Down to Earth*, London: Pratt Contemporary Art and Permanent Press, forthcoming 2008. Reprinted with the permission of the publisher.

'The Venetian Mirror' © Tamar Yoseloff. From *Fetch*, Cambridge: Salt Publishing, 2007. Reprinted with the permission of the publisher.

ʋ